It's all about IT!

It! refers to personal behaviour.
Communication is all about *it!*

🐢 **Turtle**Publishing

First published by Turtle Publishing 2024

Cover & Illustrations by Turtle Publishing

🐢 **Turtle**Publishing
turtlepublishing.com.au

Acknowledgements

There is a community of people who help us to achieve whatever it is we set out to do every day. Some of these people are close to us, and regularly catching up with them means we share all that matters. Other people have no idea that simply allowing us to sit in their café and work or clean our house gives us the freedom to do what is needed. So to all of those who have knowingly and unknowingly helped me, thank you.

For me, the never-ending support of my husband, Mark, is beyond words. We have been married for 28 years and in each other's lives for 35 years. His patience, understanding and encouragement fuel my energy to achieve my goals.

I thank my daughters, who have reviewed drafts of the book to ensure that you, as the reader, are taken through a journey that is real, relevant and applicable in your workplace.

To Dr Shaun Ridley, Dr Ross James, Evlyn Grief, Deanna Campisi—thank you for providing insights that have enabled me to grow the ideas in the book.

About the author

Dr Nancy Bonfiglio-Pavisich is a consultant specialising in leadership, management, and communication. She is the Director of Reframe WA Consulting and lives by the motto *review, renew, and regenerate.* Nancy is a passionate educator and facilitator who works with individuals, teams, and organisations to develop their respective leadership, management, and communication capacities.

Using evidence-based research, including neuroscience, coupled with mentoring and coaching, Nancy provides individual consultations, creates bespoke programs, facilitates workshops, and speaks publicly to support all stakeholders' personal and professional growth.

As a multi-award winner, Nancy has received an ACEL New Voice Scholarship Award (2020) and has been recognised with a Certificate of Excellence in Educational Leadership (2021) in Western Australia (ACELWA). Nancy's research has also seen her awarded A Western Australian Institute for Educational Research Award for Mentoring (2022) and an ACEL Fellowship Award in 2022.

Contents

What I mean

When I share my thoughts and insights about communication, I recognise that it is directed at the general population. I will do what I can to be inclusive. However, I recognise that some content (e.g. in the chapters 'Let's talk about listening' or 'Let's talk about how we speak to people') may not be relevant for some people.

When I refer to team leaders, I include those who are emerging or are in a middle leadership role that is predominantly *transactional*. A transactional leader focuses on achieving goals and fulfilling objectives. These individuals often rely on their proven skills. Their roles are operational by nature, the emphasis being the completion of tasks. The term team leader is interchangeable with managers, supervisors and coordinators.

A senior leader or executive is a role that is *transformational*. A transformational leader is focused on the big picture of the organisation and the role of the people in it. Taking risks and inspiring others to share in their vision is based on building relationships.

Introduction

It's All About It! will help you understand that communication is about a person's behaviour, not about the person. What do I mean by this?

People are people. Some days are great and others could be better. Even a friendly person might say something thoughtless or engage in behaviour that is not appropriate. For example, when chatting with a colleague, Jimmy made a condescending comment about how that colleague shared insights with the team. Despite Jimmy being aware of how much time the colleague invested in the project, the comment was shrugged off with, 'I'm only joking'. Another individual, a passionate football player in the women's league, was pleased about making the local football team. Consumed by what lay ahead, that worker's day-to-day work suffered because of constant mind wandering, internet surfing and chit-chat about her potential football career.

We accept that letting people know about the situation you are experiencing may help them to understand when you are not yourself. For example, a colleague at work had just split up from their partner of 22 years. The emotions and frustrations were evident in their day-to-day being, doing and relating.

The positive aspect of this scenario is that they told coworkers of the marriage break-up and, despite being devastated, intended to turn up to work every day in the best way possible given the circumstances, and invited coworkers to be patient for a little while.

Nothing about these situations is about the person, but everything has to do with the person's behaviour.

This book is divided into two parts. The first part (chapters one to six) examines communication and the importance of **it!**. The second part (chapters seven to nine) offers a toolkit that may help readers review their thinking, renew their approaches and regenerate action.

Introduction and chapter one

These two chapters focus on understanding the core theme of the book, which is to understand situations by removing the personal element that involves a person or personality and instead directing our focus to the person's behaviour.

Chapters two to six

These chapters explore the basic elements of communication and include the art of listening, questioning and feedback, as well as our choice and delivery of appropriate language. The chapters also introduce the concept of literacy and cultural intelligence. Understanding the language used and its delivery impacts how the message is received. In addition, I propose a model for communication that highlights the role of presence and the degree of skill required to support how information is conveyed between the sender and the receiver. Let's not forget what happens when there's a disconnect between sender and receiver. The chapter on conflict is a reminder that focusing on the **it!** and not the person makes the communication process a little easier.

Chapters seven and eight

Chapter seven has communication planning templates that have proven to be practical and effective. In chapter eight you'll find activities where you can apply what you have learned.

Chapter nine

In this chapter is a summary of the key ideas presented in the book. Here, I implore you to always defer to **it!** when navigating conversations.

I've written this book to be a simple read, reinforced with some quality tools to help your understanding of a situation before you act and to give you the courage to step up and in, and have conversations about … well, **it!**.

I encourage you to think about **it!** like this:
- Be *curious*, not *furious*.
- Be *responsive*, not *reactive*.
- Be *doing*, not *stewing*.

Chapter One

Let's talk about communication

You cannot not communicate. Every behaviour is a kind of communication. Because behaviour does not have a counterpart (there is no anti-behaviour), it is impossible not to communicate. ~ Paul Watzlawick, 2017

• • •

I refer to personal behaviour as **it!** because **it!** is what communication is all about, not the person. When we reframe our focus from the person to the behaviour, all that remains is the situation we must deal with.

I want to make it clear that focusing on behaviour instead of the person does not exonerate individuals from their responsibility. Individuals are still held accountable for their thoughts, words and actions. The emphasis here is that by focusing on behaviour (not the person) we strengthen opportunities for promoting personal and professional growth.

So, to understand **it!** (the personal behaviour), let's talk about communication.

What is communication?

Communication has existed since time immemorial. Critical for connection and understanding, both verbal and nonverbal, communication has been integral to sharing thoughts, words and feelings. Communication includes the words we choose and how we deliver them. Our facial expressions provide insight into how we feel.

Imagine if you share an idea with a work colleague and they roll their eyes at you. How would you feel? Or what about if, in your work role, you share with your team leader a concern about a situation in the team and they brush you off dismissively? How would you feel? Intention and impact are critical in this space. We must ensure that what we say and how we say something complements our intention if our message is to be understood. Equally, we must receive messages respectfully and honour the messenger even if we don't like the person delivering the message.

Communication in personal relationships

Quality dialogue is the key to successful communication in personal relationships. When we converse with others clearly and coherently, we learn about people's way of being, doing and relating. Understanding their why, their passions and their approach often provides insight into their reasons for doing what they do. Challenges occur when there is no clarity, coherence or if there is misalignment with goals—messages are misunderstood and relationships break down.

Setting clear boundaries and expectations goes a long way toward establishing mutual understanding about the relationship. For example, it's important to let people know that trust is critical to you in a relationship and, if breached, it can be a deal breaker. Equally, letting someone know that being yelled at is unacceptable also sets the parameters in a relationship.

Communication in the workplace

Human communication underpins every decision in the workplace. Quality communication is essential, whether this involves engaging in a consultation process to move the business along, establishing a positive workplace culture, and designing processes, procedures and policies.

Digital communication is another aspect that commands attention. Understanding and adapting to various digital platforms and practices is critical to communication. Being able to write an email effectively, share ideas on social media or prepare presentations requires knowledge of how **it!** can be used to ensure that our intention is aligned with our impact.

Focus on behaviour, not the person

Have you ever heard someone described as an idiot when their actions were immature? Or have you ever reacted with an expletive when driving because someone has cut in front of you? For all you know, that person is on their way to an emergency, hasn't seen you or is having issues with their car. I'm not saying that cutting in front of someone is acceptable. What I am suggesting is that it is helpful to consider the behaviour of the person—what I refer to as **it!**—and not the person. We call this approach to communication *behaviour-centric.*

Let's talk about human behaviour

A person can be defined as any entity with the moral right to self-determination.[1] The moral right refers to making life choices without harm to others. Making life choices is inherent in values, personality and character.

Because people can make self-determined life choices there is no doubt that human behaviour is complex. When we talk about human behaviour, we refer to how humans interact with one another or larger groups, interactions formed by those different life choices. Our behaviours are governed by our beliefs and values, mindset, perspectives, current and past experiences, and personal or professional pressures that are internal and external.[2]

Gabriella Philippou[3] is a psychotherapist, counsellor and trainer who writes copious articles on human behaviour. Gabriella explains that people's behaviour reflects their response to situations or environments. The factors that impact how a person responds to a situation are dependent on how well they know themselves and how well they can receive the type of message and choice of words conveyed to them. For example, someone under tremendous pressure at work due to unsuccessfully dealing with a problematic team leader becomes withdrawn and scared to share ideas about improving the organisation. Equally, a person with a forward-thinking team leader may be very optimistic in their approach and engage in risk-taking behaviour to develop products for the organisation more efficiently.

In other cases, such responsive behaviours are observable as overt actions. There are conscious actions, such as when we instinctively hug or kiss people we love when we meet and greet them at the airport. This action lets them know how valuable they are to us. Then there are subconscious actions, things we do but are unaware of. For example, I know a middle-level manager who has a subconscious habit of tapping their fingers when they're thinking—even as they're talking—and coworkers have sometimes inferred this to mean that they are becoming irritated, but they're not. Finger tapping helps them to focus, to think.

All this tells us that behaviour and personal matters are interconnected, embedded in the life experiences and identity of each person, all of which impact *why* we communicate the way we do, whether delivering it or responding to it.

Let's face it, communication can be complex, which is why it is helpful to understand the *why* of a person's behaviour, emotional intelligence, presence and communication skills. Let me explain what I mean.

The *why* of behaviour and **it!**

The *why* of behaviour is relevant to communication processes and the rationale for **it!**—the focus on the behaviour of the person and not the person.

To effectively communicate, we need to understand who we are speaking with. Simon Sinek[4] talks about understanding people's *why*. Understanding *why* is essential for anyone in a position of management. This is because people often behave in a way that is a response to specific motivations and underlying causes. For example, an individual may be traumatised from a previous work experience where they were ghosted by their team leader. They may continue to live out the experience in their memory, making them feel psychologically unsafe at a new place of work. Equally, an individual who has been in a toxic team for a long time subconsciously absorbs some inappropriate behaviours. If they get into management, it's possible that they will use those behaviours, thinking they are correct. In this situation, a team leader would need to provide them with professional learning opportunities to make them aware of their inappropriate behaviour and practice mitigation strategies.

Emotional intelligence and **it!**

As with the why of behaviour, emotional intelligence is relevant to **it!**—attention to the behaviour of the person and not the person.

To understand emotions and their impact on our behaviour, let's look at the role of the amygdala. The amygdala is located in the middle part of the brain called the limbic system. Its role is to process the emotions that humans experience, mainly the flight, fright and freeze responses. When activated, it helps us to respond to situations where we may feel unsafe. Also known as the amygdala hijack, flight, fright and freeze responses cause the brain to take control without us noticing.

In a situation where the response is physical, the amygdala sends a message to the body that may result in an increased respiratory rate and blood pressure as well as heightened alertness. For example, suppose a snake is headed in our direction. In that case, the amygdala ensures that our body responds as quickly as possible to escape harm's way. This type of response is instant. Often, we realise we have reacted after it has happened. However, the same can be said if we feel anxious or fearful about an impending conversation. We may not need to immediately jump out of the way, but the amygdala tells us there may be a potential threat. The warning means that we may need to prepare and essentially protect ourselves.

Another function of the amygdala is not always helpful. An extreme form of amygdala attack is when it goes into overdrive. We then experience acute and prolonged stress, resulting in, for example, trauma, debilitating anxiety and declining mental health. At that point, we need trained professional help that will, in a sense, create the conditions for the amygdala to tell the brain to calm down and return to its normal state.

Understanding the role of the amygdala and amygdala attack helps us to understand our own responses when we feel threatened or unsafe in some way and recognise that we might react out of all proportion to a situation or seriously overreact to someone. Understanding the role of the amygdala helps us to understand the behaviour of someone who might be overreacting in some way when we try to communicate with them.

So how do we avoid an amygdala-induced attack or overreaction? One preventative strategy is to develop emotional intelligence.

Emotional intelligence is what we bring to effective communication. In stressful situations, we can learn to manage our own emotions, relieve associated stress and develop the capacity to empathise with others and defuse conflict.

One of the leading pioneers, theorists and researchers in emotional intelligence is Reuven Bar-On, whose name is leant to a model of emotional intelligence that focuses on five areas: our skills in understanding our self-perception, self-expression, interpersonal, decision-making and stress management.[5] When aware of our emotional intelligence, we can better self-regulate our communicational responses because we know how we *turn up* for ourselves and others.

What that means is managing the attention we give to a situation—being present with a clear focus and being aware of our biases.

Presence, bias and **it!**

When I refer to **being present** when communicating with someone, I'm pointing to the need to be focused on the conversation and nothing else (in the next chapter we'll relate this to listening). Being present is determined by the capacity to manage emotions and behaviour—the **it!**—of both ourselves as the source of the communication, and the person or people we attempt to communicate with. It's a factor greatly related to the **it!** and being present makes us aware of our own biases.

Over 100 cognitive biases have been identified[6] that get in the way of seeing a situation for what it is, a symptom of amygdala attack. We make judgements about others that reflect our insecurities. Often, these insecurities cause us to personalise the problem and focus on the person, rather than focus on behaviour and the issue. Common biases include confirmation bias, negativity bias or the bandwagon effect.

Confirmation bias is precisely what it says. We tend to focus on the information that confirms our thinking (rightly or wrongly). For example, we believe that Jenny's work leaves a lot to be desired. So when Jenny cannot complete something, our notion is confirmed even when we know Jenny hasn't been given the correct data or appropriate information. In the same way, our notion of Jenny as being hopeless is confirmed if, because of our bias, we do not make an effort to find out if Jenny has been given the information or tools to complete the task properly.

Confirmation Bias

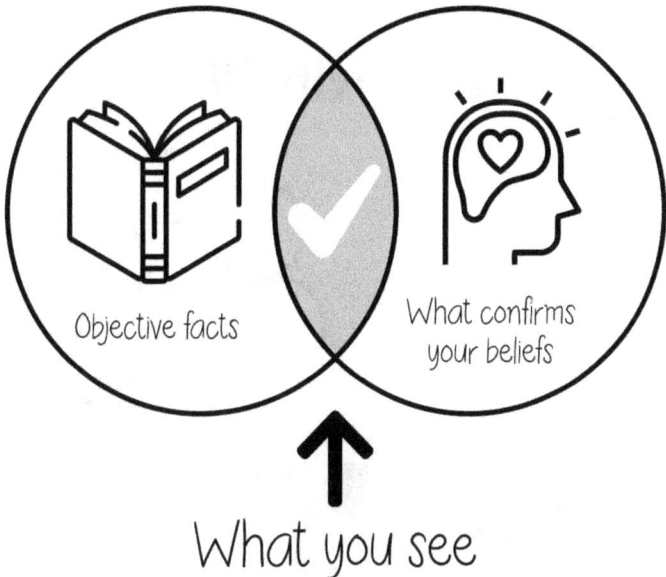

Objective facts

What confirms your beliefs

What you see

Negativity bias is another example of why we ought to pay attention to our thoughts. This bias occurs when we focus on the negative aspects of situations instead of the positive. Negativity bias is experienced by both the sender and receiver of a message. For example, when we receive feedback, despite being greatly celebrated for our work, we might focus on the information given about the one area of our work that requires improvement. Alternatively, our negative thoughts may impact how we communicate a message to others. The challenge here is to avoid negativity bias and not take personally comments about areas of improvement that might be needed, and to be sure that we avoid negativity bias when we communicate or give feedback to others.

Negativity Bias

The bandwagon effect occurs when individuals accept information provided by others without reality-testing the content. For example, you work for a high-end building company. Your boss and the leadership team visit an expo to gather insights about what can be used as a style product for your display home. Your boss hears about a particular brand of oven. He's told that all contemporary builders are buying big. Your boss asks your opinion. You don't believe the hype your boss is being told, but the boss decides to buy that oven brand and joins the bandwagon. Individuals who check the facts avoid the bandwagon effect.

The Bandwagon Effect

Being present when we turn up for others and when they turn up for us, is more effective when all parties in the communication process are self-aware of their biases. By being observant and introspective—acknowledging our thoughts, attitudes and behaviours—we are better able to attend to our biases and improve the relationships that are so important because we can better focus on the conversation.

Problem-solving skills, mindsets, curiosity and **it!**

A final factor greatly related to personal behaviour—the **it!**—that we'll touch on is the degree to which parties involved in an interaction have developed their problem-solving skills.[7]

There are far too many strategies for developing problem-solving skills for us to deal with in depth here. For the moment, I'll address two that I find helpful: a *growth mindset*, and *curiosity*. Elsewhere in this book we'll go deeper into specific strategies that support the growth of problem-solving skills such as engaging in active listening to understand and clarify issues, gathering quality feedback, carefully framing how we deliver our message, and managing conflict.

A *growth mindset* is the capacity to be observant and to be open to possibilities. A fixed mindset is the opposite. Carol Dweck[8] outlines how awareness and ongoing reflection can change people's mindsets and develop thinking that lets us see situations differently. For example, consider a performance appraisal process. A person with a fixed mindset might see the process as unfavourable and a complete waste of time. On the other hand, someone who is attentive to personal development and who has a growth mindset is likely to see the opportunity for performance appraisal as an invitation to review self and work, renew ideas and approaches, and generate new ways of being, doing and relating.

Growth Mindset

Curiosity

Presence and communication skill matrix

In this chapter we have considered the nature of communication in personal relationships and in the workplace, the why of human behaviour, emotional intelligence, presence and bias, and the development of problem-solving skills through an awareness of mindsets and being curious.

As we've seen, communication is complex! Yet human communication underpins personal relationships, community and social cohesion, and every decision in the workplace.

I've developed the presence and communication skills (PCS) matrix as a result of my experiences leading many workshops over the years. It's a helpful model to consolidate the elements of the communication process that we have briefly touched on and present them as a matrix that promotes reflection and action for improvement.

Presence and Communication Skill Matrix

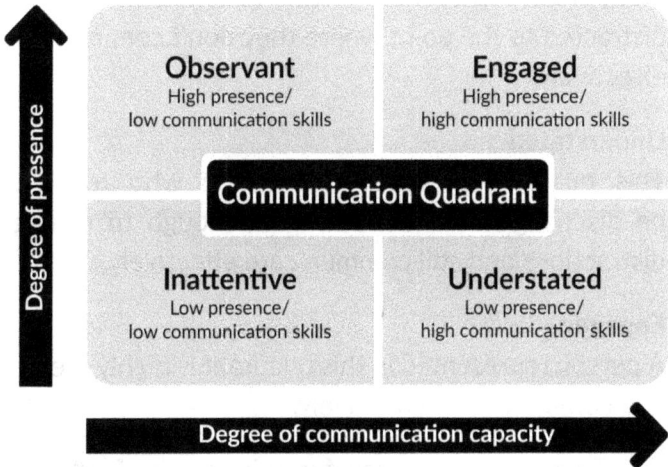

The matrix captures everything that we have considered in this chapter into degrees of presence and communication capacity or skills. Four quadrants map whether those degrees are high or low for observation, engagement, inattentiveness and understatedness.

The quadrants are an insight into the strengths and weaknesses of our communication presence and capacity.

Observant

This quadrant represents a person who is present and has low communication skills. The individual actively listens but is unable (or reluctant) to engage in the communication process.

Inattentive
The person represented in this quadrant tends to be distracted to the point where they don't communicate effectively.

Understated
This quadrant represents a person who tends to be disengaged but is self-aware enough to manage distractions and still communicate effectively.

Engaged
A person represented in this quadrant is highly present and communicates effectively.

There are two uses for this matrix. First, it is a reflection tool for reviewing how presence and communication skills impact the quality of our communication with others. Second, we can also use the matrix to determine how our communication affects those around us.

Of course, the intent of self-determining our communication capacity is to prompt a review and a plan for change and improvement.

As we have seen, communication is critical to human connection. Effective communication is all about focusing on the **it!**; the behaviour, not the person. Focusing on behaviours opens a pathway for ideas to be easily conveyed, practical teaching and learning to occur, quality decision-making made, and conflict mitigated.

The next chapter explores the art of listening to help develop sensitivity to **it!**.

Take this moment to self-reflect

Where do I fit in the communication quadrant?

What quadrant would my colleagues say I am in?

. . .

Check-in for learning ...

1. How does your learning help you to understand **it!**?

2. This chapter looked at the nature of communication in personal relationships and in the workplace, the why of human behaviour, emotional intelligence, presence and bias, and developing an awareness of mindsets and being curious. Of these, which do you identify as strengths and which do you regard as being areas for improvement?

3. In what quadrant of the PCS matrix do you perceive yourself to be located?

4. Are you present in conversations with individuals and teams?

5. How adequate is your communication capacity?

6. Why is it important to focus on understanding one's behaviour in the workplace?

7. How can the PCS matrix assist you in understanding the **it!**—an individual's behaviour at work?

8. How do you turn up?

9. How do others see you turn up?

• • •

Chapter Two

Let's talk about listening

Most people do not listen with the intent to understand; they listen with the intent to reply. ~ Stephen R Covey

• • •

Have you ever been in a situation where, although someone is speaking to you, you are so distracted by noise or other intrusions that you need to strain to listen to what they say? How did you respond? Did you tell them you were distracted or did you lie and pretend you understood what was said?

Hearing and listening are two very different approaches to giving meaning to sound.

Hearing is the first step in identifying and comprehending sounds. It is often unconscious or involuntary, with no conscious effort to interpret everything that is being heard. When you are talking with a colleague in your office, your brain is processing (hearing) background or ambient sounds such as other people talking, a chair scraping across the floor, a printer printing pages, people outside in the corridor laughing, a phone ringing in the distance. That is hearing; a physiological process that engages your brain in hearing ambient noise.

Listening is entirely different. It is the intentional and more conscious process in which the words being spoken by your colleague (and the pace and tone being used to deliver those words) are selected. Ambient or background office sounds not relevant to your foreground interaction with your colleague are deselected or pushed to the back of your mind. The process of hearing and listening is helpfully explained by Joseph DeVito's model of the five stages of listening[9] that are not necessarily sequential.

Stages of Listening

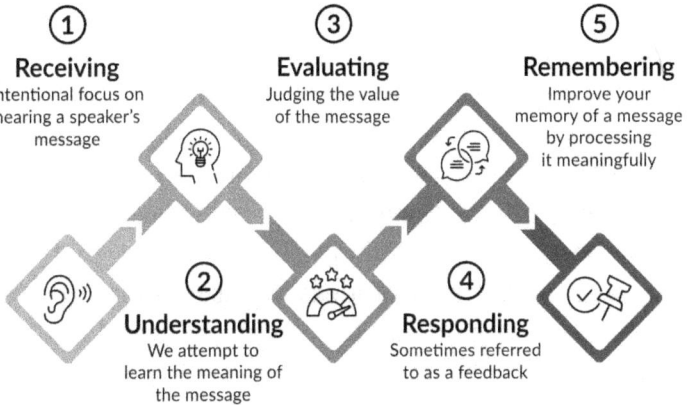

① Receiving
Intentional focus on hearing a speaker's message

③ Evaluating
Judging the value of the message

⑤ Remembering
Improve your memory of a message by processing it meaningfully

② Understanding
We attempt to learn the meaning of the message

④ Responding
Sometimes referred to as a feedback

As we listen, our brain processes the information. We are thinking about **it!** and making decisions about whether we like what we hear, how we might respond and so on.

When *receiving* information from the person speaking, we need to be present; that is, we need to be focused on the conversation and nothing else. Being focused is to take the time to process the information conveyed in order to *understand* the message. At this point, we must be mindful of our biases (confirmation bias, negative bias, and the bandwagon effect) that could get in the way of correctly processing the message.

Active listening is undergirded by asking questions (we look at that in the next chapter). Once we have actively listened and sought to understand the message, we need strategies that will enable us to **remember** the information being conveyed. We are all different in the way we remember information that is meaningful to us. Different people will remember the details of conversations differently. Some might need to remember by mentally rehearsing the information provided, others might need to consciously connect the message to something else important to them by creating patterns of ideas or associations to help remember something. The word we use for that, **mnemonic**, is the root word for memorials that we create to remember someone, such as statues or gravestones (monuments) in cemeteries.

As part of the listening process, we **evaluate** the message or information, filtered by mindset, beliefs, values, experiences. Upon evaluating the message, we now **respond** or give feedback in ways that might be positive, negative or neutral.

A positive response and feedback would celebrate the information: *'Janice, congratulations on your promotion.'*

A negative response or feedback that reflects our disappointment might be: *'Janice, I'm really disappointed about the situation. I thought there would be more options for all staff involved.'*

A neutral feedback and response adopts a neutral position, neither positive nor negative: *'Janice, I understand that you will be the new leader of the team in 2024.'*

To listen is to connect

How can we understand people's stories, share insights, learn or navigate daily situations and challenges if we don't listen? If we don't listen, we don't connect. There's an old saying that God gave us two ears, but only one mouth, and in that is a lesson. Talking is easy. Listening is a challenge.

To listen is to be present to focus on the conversation and nothing else. To listen is to be patient and refrain from interjecting or interrupting, or thinking about what we want to say while the person is speaking. There is a difference between listening to understand and listening to reply.

Effective listening also requires us to be open-minded about what is being said by being aware of our predispositions and biases. It is easy to quickly disengage when someone says something we disagree with. To listen effectively demands that we be curious, not furious, and seek to understand what is being said rather than being understood.

When we take the time to listen, we choose to understand. That's a non-negotiable, whether you are a manager or not.

Active listening

All that we have said about being present and listening is, of course, what we refer to as active listening. Intentional and deliberate, active listening enables us to better process what is being said.

Active listening has three elements: cognitive, emotional and behavioural.[10] When we talk about actively listening being *cognitive*, it means that we are actively thinking about and paying attention to the information given to us. This can also be called comprehension.

The second element of active listening, *emotional*, invites people to be aware of their reactions to what is being said. Sometimes, depending on the situation, this may look like anger or boredom.

Behavioural, the third element of active listening, refers to how we turn up to the conversation and may include how we show our interest in what is being said both verbally and nonverbally. Verbally expressed interest or feedback is done with spoken language. Nonverbal interest or feedback is through other forms of communication, most commonly facial expression, body language, or sounds such as a laugh, or a snort of derision.[11]

Some great insights into active listening come from the work of Jack Zenger and Joseph Folkman[12] who have explored listening in the workplace. They studied 3492 managers and found a difference between great and average listeners, with four focal points to good listening.

The first was that good listeners are active in the conversation process. That is, they ask periodical questions to clarify ideas and beliefs during the conversation. Second, active listening is a psychologically safe experience where the person feels supported and encouraged to share insights without fear of consequence. If someone is sharing a personal or sensitive matter relating to a coworker, a manager needs to be present and focused, listening with intent and choosing words, intonation and body language (such as facial expressions and body pose) to reflect curiosity and understanding as opposed to judgement.

A safe environment also means that the conversation is one where there is mutual reciprocity in the form of feedback. Feedback delivered in this way forms the third aspect of active listening that Zenger and Folkman align with being cooperative. The final recommendation they made is that active listeners have specialised skills that enable them to make suggestions without taking the conversation over.

Although active listening is an intricate process, disciplined practice will surely have positive outcomes when we:

- Be *curious*, not *furious*.
- Be *responsive*, not *reactive*.
- Be *doing*, not *stewing*.

Modes of listening

DeVito's model of listening explains the five stages: receiving leads to understanding, remembering, evaluation, and finally, responding or giving feedback.

As I've said already, active listening is to be present throughout those five stages of the listening process. It's being intentional and deliberate in the way we turn up to an interaction or conversation. The next few chapters look at key communication skills that help us develop the capacity for being present with intentionality, which we saw with the aid of the presence and communication skills matrix in chapter one. Here, though, we pause and ask: if those are the *hows* associated with active listening and being present, what are the *ways*?

Four modes conceptualise four ways of active listening or of being present (which is the goal of **it!**—of focusing on behaviour, not the person). The purpose and intention of each mode are explained in the following section.

Modes of Listening

Appreciative   Comprehensive   Empathetic   Evaluative

Appreciative listening

When we're in the mode of appreciative listening, we are doing so with the intention of savouring the experience. It's focusing on the enjoyment of an engaging and stimulating conversation.

Comprehensive listening

Comprehensive listening is the mode for learning. Our intention is to obtain useful information by paying attention to specific details and asking clarifying questions. Therefore, comprehensive listening must be a workplace reality in the interactions between management and staff, coworkers and colleagues in work teams (in fact, in every life situation).

Empathetic listening

When we're in the empathetic listening mode, we use it as a way of giving emotional support to the person sharing information. Here, the listening is reflective, acknowledging feelings in a safe and non-judgemental manner. We're often in empathetic mode with family and friends, in the workplace and in professional counselling.

Evaluative listening

Evaluative listening is the mode or way that we focus on making sense of the information being shared. The active listener analyses or evaluates the information through filters of mindsets, biases, beliefs and experiences. The evaluative listening mode is evident during work meetings.

What happens when we do not listen at work?

The capacity to listen is a non-negotiable skill. What if we focus on what we want and don't listen to the suggestions made by others? In that case, we risk not being trusted and supported in the vision and mission of the team or organisation. In other words, your understanding of **it!** (or lack thereof) increases the risk of not being trusted. Listening requires focus, that is, active listening.

Organisations with managers who do not listen typically have an increase in errors, loss of productivity, decreased employee engagement, and challenges aligned with staff attrition and retention.

The consequences of not listening with intentionality transgress all levels of an organisation, including how we lead our teams and how we are perceived as team leaders. It's something to think about!

As we turn to the next chapter, carry this thought: an effective listener is also an effective questioner.

Take this moment to self-reflect

How do I ensure that I listen to what is being said by my team members and by other staff at my workplace?

What strategy works well?

What do I need to do to improve?

What do I need to change?

• • •

Check-in for learning ...

1. What is the difference between hearing and listening?

2. What are DeVito's stages of listening? How can they be used to align with the listening matrix?

3. Why is listening critical to the role of an emerging or middle manager?

4. What are some listening strategies that you can use?

5. Which listening types do you use more than others?

6. How does your learning help you to understand **it!**

• • •

Chapter Three

Let's talk about questions

The master key of knowledge is, indeed, a persistent and frequent questioning. ~ Peter Abelard

• • •

Let's talk about asking questions

Have you ever asked a question and thought, Why did I ask that? What was it that I wanted to know or was hoping to learn?

Why do we ask questions? Well, with reference to the previous chapter, asking the right questions supports active listening when activated by the modes of listening.

We ask questions to 'inspire inquiry and discovery'.[13] David Fischer[14] describes questions as 'the engines of intellect' and Warren Berger[15] beautifully refers to questions as 'spades that help to unearth buried truths'.

Questions have purpose, a context in which they are used, and a required level of thinking and understanding. Mastering the types of questions and when and how to ask them will help us to understand people, think about their message, and encourage communication. Questions help us to establish a platform to foster relationships and unlock personal and professional growth.

In fact, I go so far as to say that asking questions prepares us to:

- Be *curious*, not *furious*.
- Be *responsive*, not *reactive*.
- Be *doing*, not *stewing*.

Framing questions

No matter what mode of listening we engage, questions are a part of the process of communication that enables us to understand the **it!**; the space where we focus on a person's behaviour, not the person. Questions help us to get the clarity we need to process and evaluate information and ultimately make informed decisions.

Framing a Question

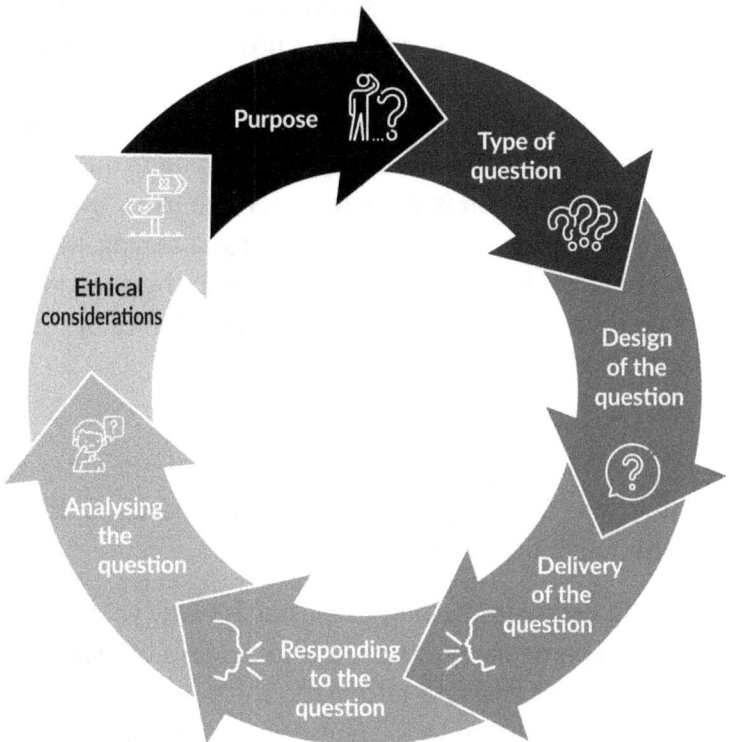

When asking the right question, we will be clear about why the question needs to be asked. Are we asking a question because we want more information, think about something more intensely or reflect?

The above illustration shows seven considerations when framing a question.

When framing a question, we need insight as to why we are asking the question. What is the purpose of the question? Once the purpose is determined, the consideration moves to choosing a type of question (e.g. whether it is convergent or divergent), designing the content for the question and then considering how to deliver that question. Interestingly, the human brain engages in the formulation of a question quite quickly. Once the question is delivered, then the focus moves to how to respond to the question by analysing what has been said. At all times, a response to the question should be respectful, ensuring that the dignity of the person is honoured.

Purpose

Questions should aim to get to the heart of **it!**; the behaviour, not the person.

To establish the purpose, establish why you want to ask a particular question. Is it to obtain a viewpoint, feelings, or facts and information? The purpose will guide the approach to the question. For example:

- Views: questions are along the lines of *'What do you think about it?'*

- Feelings: ask questions like *'How do you feel about it?'*

- Facts: these questions will be something like *'What is it?'* and *'Why?'*

Of course, questions need to be suitably framed to retrieve the information you want when you are engaged in any of the modes of active listening: *appreciative* listening, *comprehensive* listening, *empathetic* listening and *evaluative* listening.

Type of question and design

Let's begin exploring the question type and design by first looking at closed and open questions, then the questions that might apply to competitive and collaborative approaches to conversations.

Closed and Open Questions

The questions in the following table are typical of *closed*, *leading*, and *open-ended* questions.

Closed questions (convergent) have limited responses. Often the responses to closed questions consist of one word, such as yes or no, true or false. Leading questions are a type of closed question because they imply an answer; there's little room for saying much other than words of agreement.

Convergent questions are usually used to collect data or facts and are easy, quick and simple to understand.

Open-ended questions (divergent) can have multiple responses, which often furthers discussions. They are helpful for exploring and expanding on views, feelings and facts by giving details or responses.

Closed Questions (yes/no?)	Open Ended Questions (full answer)	Leading Questions (imply an answer)
Did you speak to Jim?	*What are your thoughts about the new policy?*	*You approved of the OHS policy, didn't you?*
Is that Tom's new car?	*Tell me more about the organisational restructure.*	*You did indicate that this was the course of action to take, right?*

Questions in competitive and cooperative conversations

Alison Brooks and Leslie John[16] in their article *The Surprising Power of Questions* highlighted the importance of questions in unlocking value in workplaces.

In the following two tables I illustrate how the type and quality of a question can be evidenced in a conversation continuum with a *competitive* conversation at one end and a ***cooperative*** conversation at the other, with a blend of the two conversations in between. Questions typical of competitive and cooperative conversations are shown, but the list is not exhaustive. Rather, they suggest directions that your questions could take if you recognise your conversation as being either competitive or cooperative.

Whether a question is competitive or cooperative, there are key considerations about what happens when the question is being asked or answered and the tactics used to elicit a response. As you can see, *competitive* conversations are underpinned by discussions about needs and wants. The questions are usually direct and closed. *Cooperative* conversations are different because they are naturally relational and consist of indirect, probing, reflective, hypothetical and comparative questions.

Direct Questions *(specific information sought)*	Indirect Questions *(a gentle way of seeking information)*	Probing Questions *(want to know more)*
How long have you been working for the organisation?	*I am not sure I understand. Would you be able to explain the matter to me?*	*What do the values of the organisation mean to you?*
Where did you leave the company vehicle?	*Can you tell me where the retreat area is located?*	*Can you tell me more about the challenging aspect of the situation?*

Reflective Questions (repeating information)	Hypothetical Questions (considering what may occur)	Comparative Questions (determining options)
I heard you say that the new structure would be very expensive. Is this correct?	What could be done if we were to win the contract in July?	In your opinion, which is the best pathway?
I am hearing that you are disappointed with the decision to employ John?	What would you do, if I was able to provide you with extra physical resources?	Which process will save us money?

Questions to encourage inquiry

The Greek philosopher Socrates died about 400 years before the common era, but we still use the philosopher's technique of thinking and inquiry. The Socratic method, still used in education, encourages students to work through underlying assumptions by answering thought-provoking questions or problems. This could be one way to promote the questioning process in our workplaces.

There are five stages in this process of critical inquiry: wonder, hypothesis, refutation, hypothesis acceptance or rejection, and action. Without getting into too much detail, the five stages invite people to examine a question by connecting key concepts while disputing others in order to discern the information necessary to make an informed decision. Could the Socratic method be put to work for you?

A more recent method is Warren Berger's.[17] Designed to foster creative approaches to learning and understanding situations, the Why, What if and How model introduces questions as a tool for structured problem-solving. The *Why* part of the model invites questions to help understand the problem itself. This means we gain insight into all aspects of the problem to reflect and re-examine information before moving forward. The *What if* part of the model invites the brainstorming of solutions that may solve the problem. This forms the crux of reality testing that enables us to think without constraints to see what is possible. Of course, the *How* aspect of the Why, What if, How model examines the strategies and approaches that would implement the solutions to the problem that are being considered.

Berger[18] once described the Why, What if and How model as a beautiful question asked by a three-year-old girl when the girl saw her father take a photograph. *'Why do we have to wait for the picture?'* The young child's curiosity inspired the father to ask more questions about the possibility of being able to produce prints instantly. The father of the three-year-old was Edwin Land, the person who invented the Polaroid instant camera.

What could you achieve in your workplace by asking Why, What if, How?

Delivery

The delivery of questions is about presenting or delivering the questions in such a way that they promote understanding and the exploration of the issue or matter at hand. Quality questions will be transparent, relevant and well-paced.

Our emotional state and tone of our voice as we ask a question can betray or confirm our emotions: disappointment, anger, frustration, excitement or joy.

For example, a colleague successfully gained a promotion and you didn't. The delivery made in anger will be: *'Why did they get the job and I didn't?'*

The delivery intended to promote understanding and exploration might be: *'Congratulations on your promotion'* or *'I'm not sure what I need to do to be successful in my following interview'* or *'I might connect with Tim, my team leader, and get some insights'.*

Nonverbal cues have a significant role to play in the delivery of questions and receiving responses. Eye contact, facial expressions and gestures can influence how our questions are perceived and answered. This is particularly evident when communicating with people from different cultural backgrounds. For example, making direct eye contact is offensive in some cultures. Pointing directly at someone is an insult to others. It's worth exploring culturally acceptable patterns of nonverbal cues and those regarded as unacceptable to avoid misunderstanding when there is a perceived disconnect between what is being asked and the nonverbal cues being used.

Response

When we respond to questions, we decide whether our responses will be private or transparent.

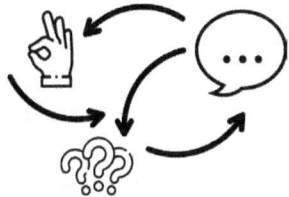

In a *private-based* response, we respond with limited information. There may be many reasons for such a response, including sharing data that might compromise a negotiation or sharing the appointment of a colleague to a position without all the protocols being finalised, which may cause human resource implications. Alternatively, *transparent* responses provide detailed information.

In the interest of developing more significant relationships, detailed responses offer a platform of openness that may assist in developing meaningful relationships. It's important to know when a private or transparent question is to be asked and in which context.

The analysis and ethics of questions

At some point, we need to analyse the question and ask: *'In asking the question, am I aware of any emotional and/or cultural implications? What is my tone like? What is my pace?'*

The analysis from an ethical perspective is a further step in deciding whether a question is to be asked or not. *'Is what I am asking relevant and appropriate for the situation?' 'How do I word the question to get a clear response?'*

Personal and professional questions are influenced by privacy and confidentiality, informed consent, and cultural and social sensitivity. The factors that impact the ethical considerations of questions include respect, truth and accuracy. Read your national, state and local legislative guidelines about what is acceptable to ask in the workplace.

The following questions are examples of questions that are loaded with ethical considerations in most workplace situations.

- *How old are you?*
- *Do you have a mental disability?*

- *Are you pregnant?*
- *What ethnicity are you?*
- *Who do you vote for?*
- *What is your sexual orientation?*

It's necessary to master the art of questioning to connect with others effectively. Asking the right questions in the right way and time can foster holistic growth. Engaging in holistic growth means that through questioning, we can better understand, navigate and effectively interact with the world surrounding us.

Take this moment to self-reflect

What are three aspects of questioning that I can embed in my day-to-day practice?

How will I know that I have done this well?

Check-in for learning ...

1. Why is the art of questioning critical to the role of an emerging/middle manager?

2. How applicable to you in your context are closed and open questions, and questions for competitive and cooperative conversations?

3. Can you use the Socratic and *Why, What if, How* questioning methods of inquiry with your team or organisation?

4. What do you need to consider when delivering your questions effectively?

5. How does your learning help you understand **it!**?

• • •

Chapter Four

Let's talk about feedback

We all need people who will give us feedback. That's how we improve. ~ Bill Gates

• • •

When you think about feedback, what comes to mind? What are examples of positive and negative feedback that you have received?

We receive feedback every single day. Whether it is verbal, physical, social or emotional, feedback offers insight into our respective capacities, reactions and sense of self.[19] Feedback is the two-way interactive process of communication by which information is shared to achieve a particular goal. When feedback is done well, it empowers people to celebrate or learn effectively and improve or change a way of being, doing and relating.

Feedback is more than a short 'well done' or 'poor work'. Whether feedback is given in our personal and professional relationships, it 'derives its value from the learning it enables'.[20]

And, of course, feedback—indeed the entire communication process—is a matter of context. The meaning of any communication is determined by context: what is said to whom, by whom, when, why and with what purpose. My intentional use of the words 'you idiot!' can have different purposes based on who I'm talking to in a specific context with a specific purpose and with a specific tone of voice.

The term feedback was used in the 1860s to provide information about the processes and practices aligned with using machinery. The term changed after WWII when it was used to provide insight into the interpersonal nature of human beings.[21]

Giving and receiving personal and professional feedback

The two-way process of feedback occurs in every context. However, the giving and receiving of feedback from other people requires care. The impact of the feedback will be determined by the quality of the relationship between the giver and receiver, the method of feedback delivery, and the environment in which it takes place.

As human beings, our insecurities and lack of skill often get in the way of quality feedback and communication. Our fears of quality feedback and communication are often based on fear of conflict, lack of understanding and cultural differences. To be effective, our feedback and communication require preparation. The process must be timely (as close to the situation as possible). It must explain what was done well or not for it to be constructive. The feedback and communication must offer encouragement, support and confidence instead of belittling someone.

Personal and professional feedback can be ***positive*** or ***negative***.

Positive feedback reinforces specific behaviours and achievements. For example: *'Jane, I was very impressed with your climate change presentation. You defined and explained climate change clearly, and accurately described the challenges that will continue to* impact our lives unless we start thinking about how we do things. Thank you.'

Negative feedback serves to develop areas for improvement. For example: *'John, I read your report about the incident. I would appreciate you providing more detail in the Incident Section so I can explain to the board what we need to do as an organisation to support the OHS requirements in the workplace better.'*

Whether feedback is negative or positive, the correct behaviour-centric approach is to be transparent, timely, fact-focused, consistent in practice and delivered with empathy.

Feedback and **it!**

The value of focusing on **it!** (behaviour associated with being, doing and relating more effectively) is that it enables us to provide feedback using appropriate communication strategies that help individuals become more self-aware about how they turn up for themselves and how others see them turn up. The process promotes the growth of relationships with the benefit playing out in workplace teams and organisations.

Effective feedback and communication ensures we focus on the **it!**, the behaviour, not the person. Known as behaviour-centric feedback, the process seeks to make individuals aware of their observable actions and how these can be modified to help their personal and professional growth. When focused on the behaviour, the **it!** becomes all-encompassing because the energy is directed away from the person to focus on the act or behaviour. Behaviour-centric feedback is specific and actionable. Its purpose is to work with facts not emotions, and pave a pathway for mutually reciprocal conversations. Essential to conveying the behaviour that has been observed or noticed are statements like these: *'Jamie, I noticed you've been late to work every day for the last three weeks. When you arrive late to work frequently, it sends a message to your colleagues that you don't value the rules that everyone must adhere to. Unless there is a specific reason of which I am not aware, I need you to arrive at work every day by a quarter past eight. If you arrive late, I'll have to initiate a performance appraisal process.'*

The feedback given to Jamie clarifies that the tardiness has been noted and will have consequences in the future.

For behaviour-centric feedback to be effective, **it!** must be used at all times. Why? Because understanding intention and impact is part of the discernment process. Of course, the behaviour can be both positive and negative.

Feedback loop

Consider a feedback loop to manage **it!**. As Elon Musk says, 'It's important to have a feedback loop, where you're constantly thinking about what you've done and how you could be doing better.'

The illustration of a feedback loop below invites reflection about the facts of the situation. A reflection of the facts also means that the person who will share information needs to ensure that their biases do not get in the way of the conversation. Their self-reflection, regular check-ins and clarification of the facts must occur before a plan of action is even considered. The emphasis here is to engage in an ongoing cycle of reflection.

- What are the facts?
- How do I know the facts to be true? (self-reflection)
- How do I check-in with self?

- What do I need to clarify?
- How will I proceed with a plan of action given what I know about me and the other person?

Feedback Loop

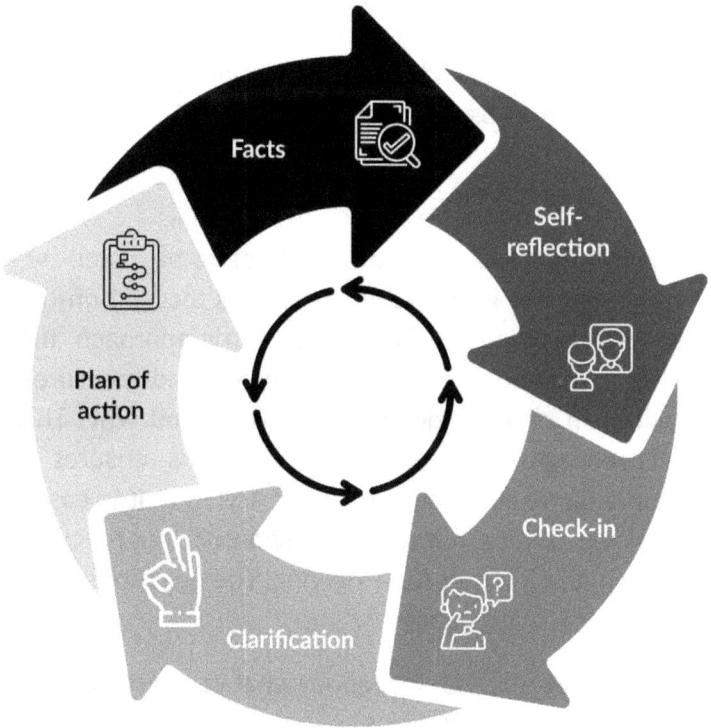

Feedback strategies

There are many and varied feedback models. As the feedback loop illustration shows, feedback is scoped and sequenced and can be used as a mechanism for reflection.

However, there are other examples of feedback strategies and I commend the following four to you: SPACT, STAR, SBI and COIN. You decide what feedback strategy works best for you.

The SPACT questions[22]

The SPACT questions are formulated to be a step-by-step guide for giving feedback that is focused on the **it!** In supporting the behaviour-centric approach, the SPACT questions invite a considered and measured reflection of what needs to be asked and why. This focused approach to asking questions ensures a scoped and sequenced course of action that is based on being curious, not furious; responsive, not reactive; and on doing rather than stewing. The questions are a checklist to focus on **it!**

- *Specific.* Be clear about what you must say and provide examples.

- *Positive–negative.* Identify the type of feedback you need to provide and consider how it may be received by the recipient.

- ***Actively listen.*** Be present as the person speaks and summarise their key points.

- ***Constructive.*** Provide feedback that provides insight into the behaviour and its consequences, as well as what needs to happen for it to change.

- ***Tailored approach.*** Know the people with whom you are communicating. Be respectful and considerate, and honour their dignity and your own throughout the process.

A behaviour-centric model begins with discussing the facts of the situation, with the behaviour in focus and not the person. For example, a direct report lied about their absence from work. They called in Friday morning at 6:00 a.m. saying that they felt sick and were too unwell to come to work. You learned there was no illness because a photograph of the direct report at the beach surfing with some friends was uploaded to Facebook.

Although the actions of the employee are disappointing, the conversation that needs to be had upon their return needs to focus on the following facts.

1. The employee called in sick on Friday at 6.00 a.m.

2. The employee went surfing.

3. A photograph was uploaded to Facebook proving it.

Team leader: *William, I want to speak with you about your absence last Friday. You called work at 6.00 a.m. informing the team that you were too unwell to come to work.*

William: *Yes. I did make the call.*

Team leader: *I noted that a photograph was uploaded to Facebook at 7:00 a.m. with you and your friends surfing at the beach. Can you tell me about that photograph?*

William: *Well, I didn't know that the photograph had been taken, so I felt better and decided to go to the beach.*

Team leader: *Given that you chose to go to the beach, I'll have to deduct your pay for Friday. You understand that sick leave is leave allocated for those who cannot be at work because they are ill. As a result of your absence, we needed to contact a relief staff member to assist us.*

William: *I'm sorry. I was feeling better, and given that I had made the call, I thought I would head off to the beach for a surf with the boys and not waste the day.*

Team leader: *Your behaviour was disappointing, William. I invite you to consider your actions and their implications for our team. As a result of the situation, I have documented the matter and have added it to your employee file. Should this occur again, you will be directed to the HR Team, who will follow up with an employee warning letter.*

An opportunity for self-reflection follows the SPACT process. During self-reflection, individuals are invited to share their feedback about the behaviour. The interviewer continues checking in with the individual to ensure the conversation remains psychologically safe. Should there be clarification of observations, then the conversation returns to self-reflection and another check-in. Once both parties are satisfied, a plan of action to mitigate change is designed and implemented, with a future meeting set for further review.

Questions or thoughts to consider for a behaviour-centric conversation with an individual—about them:

1. What observable behaviours will help support your concern or celebration?

2. What is the impact of the behaviour on yourself and others?

3. Celebrate what is done well and consider the options for change.

4. Use the art of questioning and listening to be curious and not furious

5. Honour dignity at all times—the conversation is always about personal or professional growth.

6. Ensure you regularly check in to see how the person is doing.

Questions or thoughts to consider for a behaviour-centric conversation with an individual—about you:

1. Consider you—what is your reason for speaking with the person?

2. How well do you know yourself so the conversation comes from a genuine desire to improve?

3. Choose an environment where you will not be interrupted. Ensure that the seating arrangements are as open as possible.

4. Be open to seeing the situation differently.

For example: *'Jamie, I would like to discuss how you communicate with the team. Yelling in front of the team about a task not being done without investigating why it is yet to be done makes them feel unheard and undervalued. I want to see you take the time to seek to understand the situation and then, instead of yelling at the team, gather them together and share your learnings step by step in a calm voice. Doing this will assist you in understanding the challenges facing the team and encourage the team to respect you. Should your yelling at the team continue, I'll give you a written warning.'*

The SPACT questions are examples of a toolkit resource that can be used to gauge **it!** There are examples of models that may be used in an array of contexts to help us be more curious than furious in understanding situations that arise.

Three other models of communication that may be used to assist in understanding and responding to the it! are Situation, Behaviour and Impact (SBI), the Situation, Task, Action and Results (STAR) and the Context, Observation, Impact and Next steps (COIN).

The SBI model

This three-step reflective model (created by the Centre for Creative Leadership)[23] invites the person engaging in the feedback process to address where the behaviour occurred and what it looked, sounded and felt like. The model navigates us through a tricky situation with a particular person or team, highlighting the impact of the behaviour on the relevant stakeholders.

The SBI Model

| **SITUATION** | **BEHAVIOUR** | **IMPACT** |
| Describe the situation | Describe the behaviour | What was the impact of the behaviour/ situation? |

An example of how the SBI model can work: *'Jamie, on Tuesday, when we met to discuss the Portland portfolio (**situation**), I heard you speak ill of Jason (**behaviour**) in front of the entire team. I felt disappointed because the comment was not respectful and contravened our* organisational values of honouring the dignity of the human person **(impact)**.'

The STAR model

The STAR model, from Development Dimensions International[24], is a specific feedback model. The STAR process invites the explanation of a situation and an outline of the task or responsibility that was or was not fulfilled, and concludes with the consequence clearly outlined for all stakeholders. What is significant about this model is that it helps people understand what was done well and what was not, and potentially what needs to happen to improve.

The STAR Model

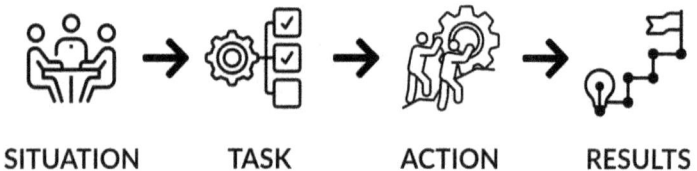

| SITUATION | TASK | ACTION | RESULTS |

An example: *At the wood plant yesterday (**situation**), I noted that the OHS procedures needed to be explicitly followed when the recruits were onboarded (**task**). Not following the OHS procedures means our recruits have not fulfilled their induction requirements correctly (**action**). The consequence is that they may need to carry out their role in a way that complies with OHS procedures (**results**).*

The COIN model

The COIN conversation model[25] is a guide that can be used to manage a feedback conversation. The conversation begins with a clear establishment of context outlining what needs to be discussed. Once the context has been established, the conversation explores what has been observed and the impact (positive or negative) it may have on specific people, teams and the organisation itself. Once the behaviour and the impact of the behaviour are acknowledged, the conversation model explores the next steps. The COIN steps may include strategies to support future practices and decisions.

The COIN Model

CONTEXT
The consideration of context invites you to think about why you would like to address the issue/situation? What needs to be discussed and Why? Provide information such as where the situation occurred, time and date etc.

OBSERVATION
Describe the actions and behaviours you observed that you want to give feedback on. Use facts. Avoid emotions and making judgements.

IMPACT
Describe the impact the actions you observed had on you and others. This can be tangible (we lost a contract) or intangible (I was upset).

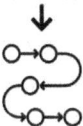

NEXT STEPS
Mutually agree on how to move forward. You may also wish to discuss how the person to whom you are speaking can engage with the process differently next time a similar situation arises.

An example:

Context: 'Michael, I want to discuss your conversation with Jane at the photocopier on Wednesday. I know the company has ongoing issues with the photocopiers. We can work together to make some arrangements.'

Observation: 'I understand that the photocopiers are jamming frequently and that this is occurring not just on our level but throughout the building.'

Impact: 'I also understand that the frequent jamming of photocopiers is causing incredible frustration for staff who want to get on with their job without having to spend lots of time attempting to mitigate the various jams that occur.'

Next Steps: 'I would like you to work with Jane and provide a proposal about the options for us, and then I would like to sit down with you both at another meeting and work through a course of action.'

Receiving feedback

It is one thing to give feedback to others, it is another when we receive feedback. Receiving feedback can be challenging.[26] Staying calm isn't always easy, mainly when the stakes are high. Being resilient is also pertinent to receiving feedback. Ensure that **individual** and **organisational** protective factors are in place. Individual factors are those that help us to mitigate situations. These include having someone to chat with or work out with, journalling, etc. Organisational protective factors are policies, practices and procedures that protect our workplace rights.

One of the key elements is to be open to the feedback (good or bad) and think about the learning coming our way. Be present and actively listen to the information to be open to learning. Learn to not interrupt (this takes some practice) and when you respond to the incoming feedback, be *curious*, not *furious*.

Another thing we can do is to ask open-ended questions that facilitate lengthy responses and details, insights and perspectives to be shared. For example:

- *What are your thoughts about the situation that occurred yesterday?*

- *I was hoping you could help me understand why the decision was not followed up with the procedure we discussed.*

- *What might be the options available to the students in the program?*

- *What should we consider to ensure that the process is effective?*

Receiving feedback isn't just about the verbal information that comes our way but also the nonverbal. Consider your body language, tone of voice and facial expressions. Once you have received the information, engage in responsive practice. It is very easy to react, but when you are responsive, you take the time to think about what is said and what you can do better.

You might wish to ask more questions at this point. Giving feedback isn't easy at the best of times, even if it is done well. Thank the person for the feedback, even if you do not agree or take any action. Critical to the feedback process is to make an action plan. Then, take the time to meet up with the person who has provided the feedback and share your insights.

Receiving Feedback

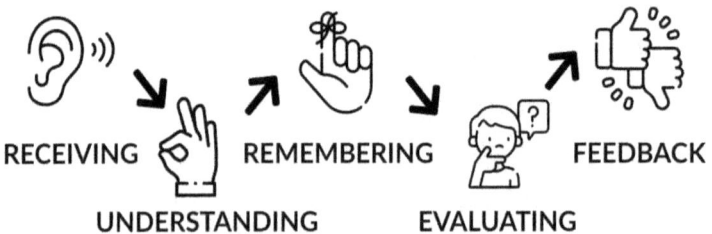

RECEIVING **REMEMBERING** **FEEDBACK**

UNDERSTANDING **EVALUATING**

Behaviour-centric feedback is a skill that can be powerful in supporting the growth of self and others. When we take the time to focus on observable actions and behaviours, we are more able to engage in quality conversations. Not commenting about the person and their traits and concentrating on the behaviour enables the feedback given to be specific and factual, allowing for productive and mutually respectful conversation.

Take this moment to self-reflect

What is it about feedback that challenges me?

What is it about feedback that comes naturally to me?

What more can I do to provide effective feedback?

• • •

Check-in for learning ...

1. Why is behaviour-centric feedback essential to the role of an emerging/middle manager?

2. What are some of the ways you can use the feedback loop in conversations?

3. Which of the feedback models works for you? Why?

4. How does learning about feedback help you to understand **it!**?

• • •

Chapter Five

Let's talk about how we speak with people

Before you speak, ask yourself if what you are going to say is true, is kind, is necessary, is helpful. ~ Bernard Meltzer

• • •

Being *curious*, not *furious* is about taking the time to get to know people, to learn about what is important to them, their values and their *why* for doing what they do. Armed with the knowledge that their behaviour does not reflect their character, we are well-placed to ask about the behaviour (the **it!**) instead of judging them personally.

Curiosity, sensitively managed, allows us to explore a situation in order to understand the reasons why that situation occurred, rather than allowing frustration to make us furious. Having a nuanced understanding of the situation promotes curiosity, compassion and a way forward to centre on behaviour, not the person.

The following chapters will expand on how to be curious by listening, asking questions, using positive feedback, carefully framing how we speak with people and dealing with conflict.

Let's talk about how we speak

'A conversation is a dance that requires partners to be in sync'. That quote from Alison Brooks and Leslie Johns[27] has to be one of my all-time favourite quotes about the reality of conversations. We all talk. The challenge is using language effectively to share our thoughts, feelings, knowledge and ideas. Being able to communicate in this way requires that we are careful how we use words. We need to appropriately select words, effectively deliver those words, and ensure that our nonverbal behaviours complement what is being conveyed.

Conversations are *formal* or *informal*. Formal conversations are determined by their settings, usually professional or official. These types of conversations are structured and follow specific rules of engagement. Informal conversations are by nature casual; they have a loose structure and include various topics. Whether conversations are formal or informal, they have similar components to consider in mastering how we speak with others.

We've already covered the dimensions of these components in previous chapters when we talked about notions of communication, listening, asking questions and feedback. Here we can cluster those ideas into a handy form that specifically relates to conversations.

Clarity
What is your message? How would you like it to be received? What do you need to consider to make this happen?

Empathy
It's critical to understand the needs of your target audience. It's essential to be present and actively listen to what is being said by promoting a mutually reflective exchange of perspectives.

Influence
Are your words and actions in alignment? One strategy to consider is being clear about people's insights and how you can positively support them.

Cultural intelligence
It's essential to be aware of and understand cultural nuances when communicating ideas. All cultures are different. Words, approaches and acceptable actions in one culture may not be acceptable in another.

Strategy

One approach to communicating effectively is to employ storytelling. Storytelling helps to set the scene or provide insight into what needs to be shared.

Literacy

People's understanding of verbal and written language is another consideration when speaking. Knowledge, skills and understanding must be shared through varied mediums so the information is conveyed in a way that suits their literacy level.

Conflict resolution

Healthy conflict is a positive way to address challenges. Having clear lines of communication and a growth mindset means conflict can be resolved by being curious and not furious.

Let's talk about tone

Communication isn't just about what you say, but how you say it!

Tone matters, as does tone mindfulness. How we deliver our message can influence the way our message is received. Tone is impacted by individual differences, contexts, and culture, and it forms part of our communication style.[28] Mary Daphne[29] points out that when neutral words are chosen but delivered with an angry, loud tone, the impact of the message changes for the listener. Communication tone is in our pitch, pace, volume and timbre.

If our *pitch* is too high, it may suggest a degree of defensiveness about an idea, process or person. Equally, a low pitch may be used to gain authority in a conversation, or it may be used to express disappointment. Be aware of the pitch you adopt in your conversations with people.

Another consideration of tone is pace. A steady, measured approach as we speak invites the listener to focus on what we are saying.

Volume will affect a listener's response to our message. If we are too loud, we may come across as aggressive and if we are too quiet, we may not be heard. The Goldilocks Principle applies here: not too fast, not too slow, but just right.

The used of *timbre* in our tone of voice is likened to the attitude that is evident when we speak. Attitude is pivotal to the message being shared because it helps the listener understand what is being said. If the timbre is one of arrogance, our message might become lost. However, a respectful and calm timbre may have more effect in expressing ideas and in having them received by the listener.

Four components make up tone, but Teresa Morell[30] explains how tone can be optimistic, pessimistic, assertive and aggressive. Some tones are more emotional than others. For example, a formal (professional) tone and an informal (casual) tone may be used in conversations. Suppose we are excited about a message we wish to convey. In that case, our voice becomes higher pitched, our volume increases, and sometimes we speak at an incredible pace. If we are not excited about our message, our pitch lowers, our volume may decrease, and we may even come across as abrupt.

Recognising that tonal shifts impact communication alerts us to tone changes, which can provide us with insight into how others are feeling. A study conducted by the University of Southern California[31] to determine how voice tone predicted whether relationships would improve. The researchers analysed recordings of conversations and focused on the various tones used between the couples. They found that the tonal characteristics of the couples predicted the journey of their relationship.

Let's talk about word choice

Choosing the right words can be tricky because our words shape our message. Our understandings and perceptions about an idea or situation are formed by the specific words used. Choice of the right words is determined by specificity and clarity[32], both of which will impact how our message is understood.

Similarly, tone and nuance provide insight into how we feel about a situation. For example, being happy about a situation differs from being excited. Happy and excited, although positive words, do not share the same intense emotion.

Cultural and social sensitivity is another consideration in word choice. Some words have different meanings in different cultures. For example, the word 'gift' in English (a present) means poison in German.

Selecting the right word has a significant impact on our day-to-day work situations. How we choose words can determine whether we are persuading or influencing people. Equally, being selective about the number of words used means that our conversations can be efficient, focused and memorable.

You are an idiot! Why did you make that decision?	*I was hoping you could help me understand what you were thinking when you made the decision.*
You have no idea! You better get your facts straight or else.	*I'm not sure you have understood the task. Let's sit down and go through it together.*
What do you do all day that gets in the way of doing your job? You are just hopeless.	*Tell me more about how you allocate your time during the day.*

Why did you do that?	*What were your thoughts when you decided to do that?*

Note the difference between these two sets of sentences and the words chosen. The idea behind this box is to showcase how we can use the **it!** in action. The left column shows a context that is personalised and quite negative. The message in the right column, however, focuses on seeking to understand the situation at hand. For example, the choice of words in the first sentence of the left-hand column is insulting. *'You are an idiot!'* There is no reason to insult someone because you do not like a decision that has been made. Alternatively, the choice of words in the right-hand column focuses on seeking to understand why a decision was taken without being insulting. Do you see the difference? Take some time to reflect on your word choices. In which column do your word choices place you?

Let's talk about engagement

Engaging people in a conversation is a refined skill. The first consideration is to know who you are speaking with and what you hope to get out of the conversation. Think about what strategy you can use to capture their attention. Consider the context, being relevant and authentic, and try to find a common starting point. For example, if you're meeting someone for the first time, you may wish to talk about your context, the weather, their sporting team, etc. Alternatively, to captivate an audience as part of a presentation, you may share a story or a thought-provoking question to connect with them emotionally. Maintaining eye contact, open body language, appropriate voice intonation, and volume are all support strategies to help you engage with those around you.

So the choice of words matters. They are merely a linchpin to establish and maintain human connection, but also an important thread in the tapestry of human relationships.

Let's talk about the connection

The words we choose impact the way we connect with people. Building a rapport will help to establish and maintain quality relationships. When we meet people for the first time the words we choose can impact the quality of our future connection. Self-regulating emotions and behaviours, facilitating understanding and engaging respectfully with people all impact relationships. Setting boundaries and clear expectations, encouraging personal and professional growth, and affirming and validating others also play a role in developing relationships with them.

Strategies for active listening

A number of strategies enable active listening, but here are six strategies that I think are worth developing. Many of the ideas have already been presented in earlier chapters. Some listening strategies will work better for you than others so select what works for you and use them!

Paraphrasing

To confirm that you have heard the information correctly, repeat the exact words used by the speaker back to them.

Ask questions

Asking questions serves a dual purpose. The first is that it may clarify ideas and information. The second is that it improves the communication experience.

Be present

When listening, ensure that the critical voice in your head (your biases) isn't getting in the way of what the person is saying. People are often so focused on their responses that they miss vital ideas expressed in the message.

Distractions

Distractions can play havoc with correctly receiving information being shared. Make sure that you are in a location away from interruptions. If you need to, place a sign on the door (Meeting in progress!) and do what you must to ensure that the other person feels safe and can have their information heard.

Be aware of your emotions

Awareness of emotions, especially when there is a high-stakes conversation in play, is critical. In this circumstance, focus on breathing and pacing your response. Ensure you repeat key ideas being shared to confirm your hearing is correct.

Nonverbal

Nonverbal feedback helps the person speaking feel that they are being heard. Nodding, eye contact, attentive facial expressions, and posture are physical behaviours that show our interest.

Take this moment to self-reflect

How would I describe the way
I speak to people?

What works well for me?

What are some things I need to think
about when speaking to people?

• • •

Check-in for learning ...

1. Why is the art of speaking a critical skill for an emerging/middle manager?

2. Which of the four components of tone do you need to focus on when talking to others?

3. Are you confident in your ability to choose the right words to facilitate engagement and connection? What do you need to change to improve?

4. Which of the strategies for active listening come easily to you, and do you use them often? Which ones could you work on to improve active listening?

5. How does your learning help you understand **it!**?

• • •

Chapter Six

Let's talk about conflict

For good ideas and true innovation, you need human interaction, conflict, argument, debate.
~ Margaret Heffernan

• • •

Conflict is a natural part of the communication experience. How conflict is dealt with determines the outcome of a situation. For this chapter, we will use the definition of conflict outlined by HDRQ[33]: 'conflict occurs when parties with contrasting goals, values or attitudes come in contact with one another'. The environment in which communication takes place also has an impact on conflict.

Think about a time when you have been involved in conflict. What was the conflict about? Were you able to resolve it? If so, what did you do? If not, what could you do better next time?

History of conflict

Plato and Aristotle first documented our understanding of conflict. Both philosophers agreed that the root cause of conflict was the 'flaws of character in individuals or unintelligent political arrangements'.[34] We'll leave their comment about political arrangements for others to dissect in-depth and satisfy ourselves with a summary of their views. They argued that the only way conflict could be resolved was to implement some form of order because—for centuries—conflict was determined to be evil. If it couldn't be avoided at all costs, then it needed to be removed with great expediency when it did occur.

It took a long time for people to think about conflict differently but a new idea emerged in the 1960s. Although there is no doubt that conflict had adverse outcomes, leaving those involved in the process feeling upset and disillusioned, it came to be accepted that the human condition would always be aligned with conflict and is characteristic of the differences that we have as human beings.[35] Accepting that there would always be differences in perspectives, attention moved to understanding conflict styles. We'll talk about this a little later.

The nature of conflict

Healthy and harmful conflict

Healthy conflict is a constructive and respectful conversation that invites participants to openly share perspectives and continue to respect and honour the other person's dignity. Also known as positive conflict, healthy conflict focuses on the issue (about **it!**), not the person. It is based on mutually reciprocal and accountable relationships. Those relationships have clear boundaries that enable people to express ideas and opinions in open conversations or interactions that are honest, flexible, reflective and responsive.[36]

Harmful conflict is about disagreements between parties with different and non-negotiable viewpoints. These types of conflict occur, sadly, far too often in interpersonal, organisational, community or international relationships. Harmful conflict—or destructive, negative conflict—wreaks havoc in relationships when it is a personal attack that is aimed at the person, the individual's personality traits, and not the behaviour. Harmful conflict results in distrust, lack of commitment and poor accountability, all of which can impact the outcomes of projects. Fuelled by poor communication, a lack of resolution and hostile behaviour, the consequences of negative conflict can be catastrophic. A helpful focus for managing conflict is to:

- Be *curious*, not *furious*.
- Be *responsive*, not *reactive*.
- Be *doing*, not *stewing*.

The source of conflict

From the perspective of interpersonal relationships, a source of conflict may be connected to relationship challenges with miscommunication, ineffective listening or differences in beliefs and values. In a professional context, the source of conflict can be interpersonal challenges, power dynamics, limited resources, systems and processes, and economic complexities. A critical process of the **it!** is to identify the source of a conflict and then determine a strategy to help resolve it.

Our brain responds to conflict because it is intrinsically wired to respond to danger. In chapter one we saw that the amygdala, which processes emotions, is located in the limbic system, the part of the brain where we feel. When we are feeling frightened, the amygdala activates a response of either flight, freeze or flight. And so, we realise that when we sometimes react instinctively and perhaps unconsciously, the suddenness of that action or instinctive behaviour to take flight, freeze or fight, can affect the conversation we're having with someone.

Even as the amygdala engages in a protective mode, the brain itself engages in a process of thinking that creates shortcuts. These shortcuts are aligned with what we call cognitive biases. Alicia Nortje[37] wrote an article for **Positive Psychology** and explained that cognitive bias is a way of thinking, doing and being that can impact the way we deal with scenarios that affect us daily.

There are over 180 cognitive biases. **Confirmation bias** is when we look for data or people who confirm our beliefs and expectations. For example, sales figures are used to support the profit and loss spreadsheet. **Gender bias** is when we focus on specific behaviour traits and qualities that people perceive as being aligned with gender.

Not all cognitive biases are right nor are all of them wrong because they are a product of experiences. It's important to be aware of the why, the how, the what and when that leads to our decisions and learn and seek to understand the viewpoints of others.

Conflict types

Multiple levels of conflict are defined by the degree of their intensity and complexity and the context in which the conflict occurs. The classifications of conflict in the illustration below help us to understand conflict contexts and how to address them from the perspective of **it!**, in which we focus on the behaviour, not the person.

Classifications of Conflict

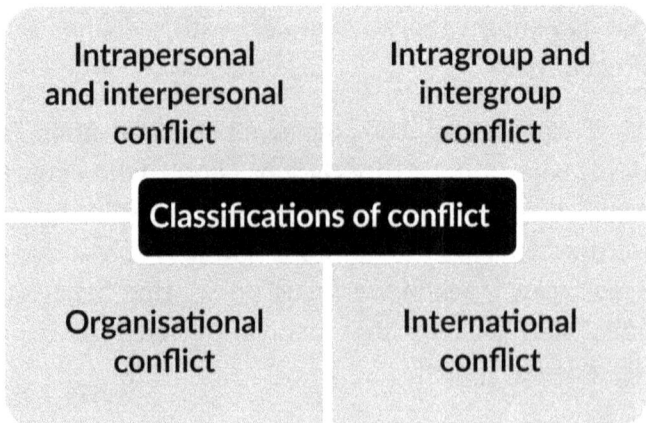

Intrapersonal and interpersonal conflict	Intragroup and intergroup conflict
Classifications of conflict	
Organisational conflict	International conflict

- *Intrapersonal conflict* refers to conflict with self, resulting from the emotions, values and choices one needs to make. For example, someone has difficulty accepting an invitation to a former partner's party, or another may find it challenging to have a friendship with the family of an ex-partner. These types of conflict test our values, beliefs and mindsets.

- *Interpersonal conflicts* occur between two or more people. The disagreements vary from personal to professional matters. For example, a dispute between two coworkers about how a particular task needs to be completed, or a situation where a manager struggles to implement change within their team can also reflect salient interpersonal conflict.

- *Intragroup conflict* occurs within a group. *Intergroup conflict* is between two or more teams or groups. Both these types of conflict, common in workplaces, can be sourced in competition, limited resources and personality clashes. Competing teams may have different perspectives about a specific solution to a problem, which causes them to focus on people instead of **it!**.

- *Organisational and international conflict* occurs when a large number of people are disconnected. The degree of disconnect can be linked to policies, practices, ideology and territorial matters. Common to all is a disconnect in values, opinions and approaches. What is pertinent in understanding conflict is that any level of conflict requires skill to manage it. This includes selecting appropriate strategies and resources to mitigate a mutually beneficial and effective resolution.

Conflict levels

Personal and professional conflicts that occur daily can be conveniently grouped into the levels of **relationships**, **tasks** and **processes**.[38] A dispute in a relationship, whether personal or professional, is sourced in different values and competing interests that get in the way of communication. The challenge here isn't limited to the conflict between two people but also involves the 'emotional shrapnel' that is experienced by those individuals who know and work with those who are in conflict.[39] Obviously, conflict relating to tasks and processes is sourced from the different perspectives and experiences that group members have and their views about how a task and the procedures should be undertaken. This type of conflict, especially in the workplace, must be carefully managed to avoid impacting productivity and the bottom line.

Think about your workplace. What are the types of conflict that you see and hear about? What do you think needs to happen to mitigate the frequency and types of conflict?

Conflict styles

Conflict styles are underpinned by *negative* and *positive* *mindsets*.

Negative ways of managing conflict are to avoid it, accommodate it or confront it. Avoidance as a practice is used to circumvent a situation, such as avoiding someone by looking the other way. Alternatively, being accommodating means that a person can place the concerns of others at the forefront and not their own. For example, James and John are working on a project with a very short deadline. The short deadline means that both parties need to work overtime. James has a family and has asked John if they could work after eight o'clock at night, Monday to Thursday, so that their children can be put to bed. For John, this means not being able to play team basketball. John accommodates James's request at a personal cost.

Alternatively, Megan and Jane have each designed a strategy that will ensure the organisation is able to meet a contract deadline. The challenge is that only one can be presented at next Monday's meeting. After much discussion, Jane steps back to accommodate Megan's desire to present her strategy.

A confrontational approach as a conflict style can be harmful, especially when people adopt aggressive behaviour. For example, Michael is very angry at having been informed that Liang has made a complaint about him. Instead of staying calm and organising a time to meet Liang, he rushes over to him and verbally threatens him.

Negative conflict styles do not support an understanding of the **it!**.

However, positive—or healthy—conflict styles invite us to be open-minded and flexible in agreeing on a solution. Examples of positive or healthy conflict approaches include *cognitive adaptability*, *collaboration* and *compromise*. Cognitive adaptability is about ongoing reflection, strategic planning and flexibility, all responses that are open to possibilities.[40] An employee shows cognitive adaptability after putting forward a meticulously planned proposal for change within the organisation only to be told that the situation is now different. Instead of getting frustrated or taking the feedback personally, the employee engages in an inquiry process to reconfigure the proposal to better meet the needs of the team.

Collaborating conflict styles make it possible for people to work together to solve a particular challenge. For example, two competing project teams may decide that working together will assist them in achieving a well-designed product. Compromising is another positive conflict style that seeks a common understanding for mutual satisfaction. In this circumstance, identifying essential goals becomes the focal point of an arrangement instead of self or group interest. Compromising as a conflict style focuses on the mutually reciprocal process of all stakeholders benefiting from the decision made. Win-win!

What about you?

Show me a group of humans and I'll show you the potential for conflict! Our part is to know ourselves well enough to understand what triggers our response and to respond respectfully by placing the **it!** at the forefront. Navigating conflict conversations with will and skill means listening, asking questions, reflecting and learning, which are part of the makeup of a conflict resolution style that is being curious, not furious.

Conflict involves consideration of not only another party but also ourselves. Are you self-aware? What is your likely contribution to a conflict? What biases do you have? What is it about the situation that triggers you? How can you ensure you respond (with thought and skill) instead of reacting? Once you have addressed these questions, consider which quadrants below reflect the approach required to manage conflict. Consider your degree of self-awareness in light of the degree to which you respond to conflict situations.

And just a reminder: conflict mitigation is possible if we:

- Be *curious*, not *furious*.
- Be *responsive*, not *reactive*.
- Be *doing*, not *stewing*.

Problem Identification Matrix

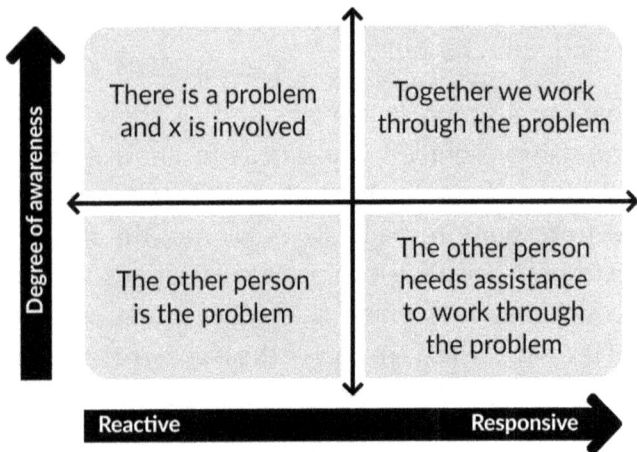

Human beings are different. What one person may deem to be a problem, another may not. The problem identification matrix invites us to think about how we understand a situation of conflict. To do this, give attention to whether there is a belief or facts to indicate that there is a problem.

For example, the top left-hand quadrant invites us to acknowledge there is a problem and a specific person is involved. What is our thinking here? Do we consider our cognitive bias to ensure that we are not using a situation as evidence to support our perspective of someone? Are we being reactive? Alternatively, do we consider the approach offered in the top right-hand side of the quadrant? The degree of awareness highlights there is a problem but instead of focusing on the individual, the focus becomes the **it!**. Once the **it!** is determined, the attention moves to how to mitigate the situation in a responsive way.

Think about two situations. In the first situation, how did your degree of awareness result in a reactive response? In the second situation, think about how your degree of awareness resulted in a responsive approach.

What can be done when negative conflict is in play?
Several strategies can disrupt negative conflict. First, seeking to understand before being understood (Stephen Covey[41]) is essential. Try and see the situation from the perspective of the other. Focus on the **it!**. *How*, might you ask?

First, you may want to understand how the person feels about the situation. It would help if you acknowledged how the person is feeling. Active listening without interruption enables each party to share their respective perspectives. When we listen, we are better able to discern the **it!**.[42] Secondly, finding common ground, although tricky, helps them to know that you understand some of the concerns they may have. Acknowledging the **it!** and creating a space for the matter to be resolved in an open, non-blame-based approach helps to grow relationships. Staying calm, being empathetic, having the skill to self-regulate behaviours, and adopting a problem-solving mindset may assist in curtailing the negativity of the situation by focusing on the **it!**.[43]

Remember, by being curious and not furious, we invite the art of questioning to help us understand the facts of the situation. Asking questions enables us to think. The process buys us time to explore the issue instead of simply reacting without thought. This involves being responsive and not reactive. Being curious and not furious also invites people to engage with the situation to want to know more **it!** instead of stewing on assumptions, inferences or even the wrong information!

Take this moment to self-reflect

How do I handle conflict?

What works for me? What does not work for me?

What could be improved?

What is it about feedback that
comes naturally to me?

What more can I do to provide
effective feedback?

. . .

Check-in for learning ...

1. Why is managing conflict critical for an emerging/
    middle manager?

2. How might you use the problem identification
    matrix when determining a potential conflict?

3. How does your learning help you understand **it!**?

•   •   •

Chapter Seven

Communication tools

• • •

Communication Plan

To understand the **it!**, create a communication plan for a process and appropriate strategies to direct a conversation away from the person and straight to the behaviour or the it!. You will recall in chapter one we discussed the importance of removing the personal element in a conversation. Similarly, in chapters two to six, we explored the basic elements of communication as well as the concepts of literacy and cultural intelligence.

In this chapter, I have provided you with examples of communication tools that support the content covered thus far. The first communication tool (template one) provides you with a checklist of what to think about before having a conversation with someone.

Consider a meeting plan that is designed to help you think about why you are meeting the person and invites you to set a goal. It also invites you to think about the timing, the strategy you choose and the potential for challenges. The tool is also useful to keep you in check as you have the conversation.

Communication tool one

MEETING PLAN	
Goal	
Target audience	
Roles/ responsibilities	
Situation	
Timing	
Strategy	
Potential challenges	
Review / feedback	

If the above communication tool does not work for you, consider communication tool two. This tool clusters the thinking, doing and relating aspects of the situation and potential conversation into three components: situation, action and outcome. The principle behind this simple process is to be curious rather than furious and to be responsive rather than reactive.

Communication tool two

Situation, action, outcome

SITUATION
What is the situation? What are the facts? Have you tested the reality of those facts? NOTES...

ACTION

What are the options available to you? What needs to happen?

NOTES...

OUTCOME

Once you have identified the action to be taken, map out the potential scenarios that may result. Which one of these are you comfortable adopting? What do you need to do to make the adopted option occur?

NOTES...

The third communication tool provides you with a guide to keep meeting details in check. Focusing on and capturing the relevant details of a conversation ensures that there is clarity, consistency and follow-up.

Communication tool three

TEAM COMMUNICATION LOG		
Team name		
Swing A/B		
Type of communication	❑ Daily	❑ Weekly
	❑ Toolbox	❑ Monthly
	❑ One on one	❑ Team
Discussion Items		
Action		
Follow Update		

Another example of a communication tool is a well-thought-out and communicated agenda. Here is a guide to ensuring that all stakeholders have a seat and voice at the meeting. There should be clear structures, processes and practices in place to ensure that the operational aspects of the agenda are adhered to in meetings. Once effectively implemented and communicated, the operational aspects of the agenda pave the way for ideas to be presented, debated and actioned.

Communication tool four

Agenda

Before the scheduled meeting you may wish to consider the following four steps.

Step one

- Seek input from the respective stakeholders about what must be discussed at the meeting. This may be done verbally or in writing. Be sure to capture everything.

- Collate all ideas and categorise them. Consider whether the agenda items can be quickly addressed away from the meeting. Only place items on the list that are pertinent and require that all members of the team know about them.

Step two

- Formulate the agenda, paying attention to the time required for each agenda item and who will speak to each item.

- Consider all stakeholders.

- Determine time and place.

- Establish a structure for the meeting and ensure all stakeholders are informed.

Step three (at the meeting)

- Review the meeting structure before you begin.

- Use a timer to keep those presenting a topic in check.

- Take minutes.

Step four

- Send minutes to all stakeholders.

• • •

Chapter Eight

Your turn

• • •

Knowing what you now know, how will you step up and into conversations to ensure you focus on **it!**? Have a go at working through the scenarios provided.

Scenario one

You need to check in with a colleague about a concept or idea. You are feeling inadequate because you know they tend to be critical. You also understand that if you do not include them in the consultation process, everyone in the office will hear about it.

Think about the type of conversation you might have. *What will you consider? Of the approaches, models* and tools presented in previous chapters, which one (or more) is likely to be of use in this situation?

Scenario two

John is an executive lead who is very career-focused. You know John likes to take other people's ideas and make them their own. As a dedicated project manager, you see an opportunity to change the performance metrics used to measure the critical aspects of the Drilling Port Code project. Ideally, you would like to keep John out of the project. However, you do not have a choice.

Be creative. *How will you approach the conversation with John? What will you consider? Of the approaches, models and tools presented in previous chapters, which one (or more) is likely to be of use in this situation?*

Scenario three

Jenny is the ultimate perfectionist and is supersensitive, yet colleagues in the business trust and respect Jenny. You are concerned that Jenny spends too much time on the monthly reports. Stakeholders are concerned that although the reports received are faultless, they do not have enough time to review them for the next meeting.

How will you approach this conversation with Jenny? What will you consider? Of the approaches, models and tools presented in previous chapters, which one (or more) is likely to be of use in this situation?

Scenario four

The organisation is seeking to redefine its training process. One of the decisions made by the executive is to rotate all managers through the various team roles. You have been asked to go back to a role that you have previously filled. You are reticent about the prospect of doing so because you have had to handle the existing team before and it was a challenging task. Even though you mitigated all the challenges with great success, you are burned out and feel that going back will cause you a lot of stress.

How will you approach this conversation? What will you consider? Of the approaches, models and tools presented in previous chapters, which one (or more) is likely to be of use in this situation?

Scenario five

You are undergoing a performance appraisal process. Company policy requires this to be undertaken on an annual basis. Although you have no issue with the appraisal itself, you are very concerned about the team leader who is facilitating the process. You know the team leader's reputation for cronyism and for trying to find ways to get a close mate to join the office. You are feeling anxious.

How will you handle this conversation? What will you consider? Of the approaches, models and tools presented in previous chapters, which one (or more) is likely to be of use in this situation?

Scenario six

You are a female team leader who works at a grain collection point in a regional country town. Today is a busy day, and you and your female team must move 10 chutes within one hour. Just as you and your team are about to lift the first chute, Jason shouts out, 'Don't do that! Us boys have it.' Before you know it, Jason and Jason's mates have pushed in and taken over.

How will you approach this conversation? What will you consider? Of the approaches, models and tools presented in previous chapters, which one (or more) is likely to be of use in this situation?

Scenario seven

For you, going to work every day is a joy. You love the work you do, and you are acknowledged for it. Of late, you have noticed that your team leader is giving you extra work. At first, you thought it was a one-off, but after three weeks, you realise that it is getting harder to complete your job because of the new workload.

How will you approach this conversation? What will you consider? Of the approaches, models and tools presented in previous chapters, which one (or more) is likely to be of use in this situation?

Scenario eight

On Friday you were informed of a work event that half of the organisation's staff was invited to attend. At first, you thought this was an error. After conversations with other staff on Monday, you realise that some teams were intentionally not invited to mitigate costs. You decide that you need to speak to a member of the executive team.

How will you approach this conversation? What will you consider? Of the approaches, models and tools presented in previous chapters, which one (or more) is likely to be of use in this situation?

● ● ●

Chapter Nine

Let's talk about how it! comes together

• • •

We make a choice every time we engage in communicating with others. Being present with skill is critical in understanding the *why* of people's behaviour.

it! brings attention to the communication process. **it!** is about the behaviour. Focusing on the behaviour rather than the person is essential to communicating effectively.

Using a behaviour-centric approach offers a pathway for interaction that promotes a greater understanding of a situation. In seeking to understand true intent, we gain insight into the thinking and emotion that has driven the action. In fostering a greater understanding of the situation, a behaviour-centric approach assists in developing healthy relationships. Why? Because the approach fosters greater insight through active questioning, listening and feedback. It helps us to be *curious*, not *furious*, *responsive* not *reactive*, and *doing*, not *stewing*.

Chapter one introduced us to understanding behaviour. The chapter examined the role of the amygdala in actioning a response to situations. The flight, fright and freeze response helps us to protect ourselves. Understanding our emotions and the way we manage our attention is pertinent to the process. Being emotionally intelligent means that we are better able to self-regulate when the amygdala hijacks our senses, causing us to react rather than respond to the matter at hand. We also explored cognitive biases and how these can get in the way of our thinking and ultimately our decision-making process.

Chapter two made us aware of the difference between hearing and listening. The brain processes the sounds that surround us; that's hearing. Giving attention to what is being heard and processing it is listening. We looked at the stages involved in the listening process and examined several strategies to assist you in listening with focus.

Chapter three delved into the art of questioning. Learning about the two main types of questions, *convergent* and *divergent*, enabled us to appreciate the thinking required in sending and receiving messages, particularly paying attention to the word choices and delivery of our questions. Asking the right question goes a long way to finding quality answers.

Chapter four was all about feedback. Often, we are asked or are required to provide individuals and organisations with quality feedback. The chapter explored the key criteria aligned with feedback and invited you to examine several models that may support you in the conversations you have.

Chapter five directed our attention to how we speak. Our tone and body language are components of communication that, when used well, ensure our message is being conveyed. When our tone and body language are not in alignment with our words, a disconnect results in the message being misunderstood by the receiver.

Chapter six was dedicated to understanding the conflict that may potentially arise when we do not communicate effectively. Understanding the nature and source of conflict goes a long way in helping us determine the strategies we need to adopt to ensure the conversation is responsive (with thought) and not reactive (by emotion). When we respond, we are thinking about what we are saying. We are clear about our why and have thought through the choice of words, tone and the delivery of the message. When we do not think about our response, our reaction severely disrupts our message.

Chapter seven provided several tools for you to consider when planning upcoming conversations.

Chapter eight invited you to apply the knowledge presented in the book to various situations that have been kindly shared by participants in my workshops.

Now, ask yourself:

What do you need to focus on to assist you to better understand **it!**?

- Do you need to engage in regular reflection?
- Do you need to become more self-aware about how you turn up for yourself and others?
- Do you need to listen more than hear?
- Do you need to ask the right question?
- Do you need to evaluate your choice of words, tone and the overall delivery of your message before you begin to speak?
- Do you need to think about what conflict looks, feels and sounds like for you? What strategies might you consider to ensure that you engage in healthy conflict?

Whatever you need to do to make you a better communicator, do **it!**

Reframe, renew and regenerate your approach to situations by focusing on the **it!** because **it!** goes a long way in engaging in and maintaining healthy relationships.

• • •

Endnotes

Chapter One

1   David Leech Anderson n.d.

2   Zipf, G. K. (2016). *Human Behavior and the Principle of Least Effort: An Introduction to Human Ecology.* Ravenio Books.

3   Philippou, G. Human behavior in the workplace. https://gabriellaphilippou.com/human-behavior-in-the-workplace/

4   Sinek, S. (2011). *Start With Why.* Penguin Books.

5   Stein, S. J., & Book, H. E. (2011). *The EQ Edge: Emotional Intelligence and Your Success.* John Wiley & Sons.

6   Ehrlinger, J., Readinger, W. O., & Kim, B. (2016). Decision-making and cognitive biases. *Encyclopedia of mental health*, 12(3), 83-7.

7   Krogerus, M., & Tschäppeler, R. (2018). *The Communication Book: 44 Ideas for Better Conversations Every Day.* Penguin UK.

8   Dweck, C. S. (2006). *Mindset: The New Psychology of Success.* New York Random House Publishing Group. References Scientific Research Publishing (scirp.org).

Chapter Two

9   DeVito, J. A. (2000). *The Elements of Public Speaking (7th ed.)*. New York, NY: Longman.

10   Abraham, R. & Groysberg, B., (2021). How to Become a Better Listener. **Harvard Business Review online.**

11   Donald K. Smith has detailed in his book, *Creating Understanding* (1992), the 12 signal systems that the world's cultures use to communicate, but differently, with different meanings. There is, of course verbal (speech), however the 11 nonverbal signal systems are: written (symbols that we use to represent speech), numeric (numbers), pictorial (drawings and paintings), artifacts (things we create and use), audio (nonverbal sounds—and silence!), kinesics (body language, facial expressions, posture), optical (light and colour), tactile (how we touch), spatial (how we use spaces), temporal (the use of time), olfactory (taste and smell).

12   Zenger, J., & Folkman, J. (2016). What Great Listeners Actually Do. *Harvard Business Review*,14.

Chapter Three

13   Seyferth, A., Ratna, A., & Chung, K. C. (2022). The Art of Questioning. *Plastic and Reconstructive Surgery*, 149(5), 1031-1035.

14 Fischer, D. H. (1970). Historians' Fallacies: Toward a Logic of Historical Thought.

15 Berger, W, (2016). *Fast Company.* How Brainstorming Questions, Not Ideas, Sparks Creativity. Available at: www.fastcompany.com/3060573/how-brainstorming-questions-not-ideassparks-creativity Accessed 25 October 2023.

16 Brooks, A. W., & John, L. K. (2018). The Surprising Power of Questions. *Harvard Business Review*, 96(3), 60-67.

17 Berger, W. (2016). *A More Beautiful Question: The Power of Inquiry to Spark Breakthrough Ideas.* Bloomsbury Publishing USA.

18 Berger, W. (2014) A More Beautiful Question. Interviewed by Larry Ferlazzo. https://www.edweek.org/teaching-learning/opinion-a-more-beautiful-question-an-interview-with-warren-berger/2014/07 (edweek.org).

Chapter Four

19 Sutton, R. M., & Douglas, K. (2010). *Feedback: The Communication of Praise, Criticism, and Advice.* Peter Lang. (Leary and Terry cited in Sutton and Douglas, Interpersonal aspects of receiving evaluative feedback).

20 Brookhart, S. M., & McMillan, J. H. (2020). *Feedback and Measurement. Classroom Assessment and Educational Measurement*, 9780429507533-5.

21 Stone, D., & Heen, S. (2015). *Thanks for the Feedback: The Science and Art of Receiving Feedback Well*. Penguin.

22 Gambill, T., (2021) The Art of Asking Higher Quality Questions. *Forbes Magazine*.

23 Bommelje, R. (2012). The Listening Circle: Using the SBI Model to Enhance Peer Feedback. *International Journal of Listening*, 26(2), 67-70.

24 Development Dimensions International. The STAR Model. https://www.ddiworld.com/solutions/behavioral-interviewing/star-method

25 Carroll, A. (2014). *The Feedback Imperative: How to Give Everyday Feedback to Speed Up Your Team's Success*. Greenleaf Book Group.

26 Jug, R., Jiang, X. S., & Bean, S. M. (2019). Giving and Receiving Effective Feedback: A Review Article and How-To Guide. *Archives of pathology & laboratory medicine*, 143(2), 244-250.

Chapter Five

27 Brooks, A. W., & John, L. K. (2018). The Surprising Power of Questions. *Harvard Business Review*, 96(3), 60-67.

28 Gottman, J., & DeClaire, J. (2002). *The Relationship Cure: A 5 Step Guide to Strengthening Your Marriage, Family, and Friendships.* Harmony.

29 Daphne, Mary., Columbia University Ed.M., Communication and Linguishes, YouTube, retrieved from .https://youtu.be/h3d34;AsdFk

30 Morell, T. (2015). International conference paper presentations: A multimodal analysis to determine effectiveness. *English for Specific Purposes*, 37, 137-150.

31 University of Southern California. (2015). Words Can Deceive, But Tone of Voice Cannot. *University of Southern California.* https://today.usc.edu/words-can-deceive-but-tone-of-voice-cannot/

32 Kahneman, D. (2017). *Thinking, Fast and Slow.*

Chapter Six

33 Human Resource Development Quarterly (HRDQ). (2013). *Conflict Strategies Inventory—facilitator's guide.* (3rd Ed). United States of America.

34 Skultety, S. (2019). *Conflict in Aristotle's Political Philosophy.* State University of New York Press.

35 Rahim, M. A. (2023). *Managing Conflict in Organizations.* Taylor & Francis.

36   Gallo, A. (2022). *Getting Along: How to Work with Anyone (even Difficult People)*. Harvard Business Press.

37   Nortje, A. (2020). What Is Cognitive Bias? 7 Examples & Resources (Incl. Codex). *Positive Psychology.com* https://positivepsychology.com/cognitive-biases/ accessed 30 October 2023

38   Human Resource Development Quarterly (HRDQ). (2013). *Conflict Strategies Inventory—facilitator's guide.* (3rd Ed). United States of America.

39   Gallo, A. (2022). *Getting Along: How to Work with Anyone (even Difficult People)*. Harvard Business Press.

40   Haynie, J. M., Shepherd, D. A., & Patzelt, H. (2012). Cognitive Adaptability and an Entrepreneurial Task: The Role of Metacognitive Ability and Feedback. *Entrepreneurship Theory and Practice*, 36(2), 237-265.

41   Covey, S.R.(2020). *The 7 Habits of Highly Effective People.* Simon and Schuster.

42   Bregman, P. (2012). *How to Respond to Negativity.* Harvard Business Review.

43   Seppala, E., & Bradley, C. (2019). *Handling Negative Emotions in a Way that's Good for Your Team.* Harvard Business Review.